BETHANY KEY

HOW TO DEFEND YOURSELF FROM NARCISSISTIC AND TOXIC PEOPLE

The ultimate guide to learning how to protect yourself from manipulators and stop being manipulated.

© Copyright 2021 - All rights reserved.

The content contained within this book may not be reproduced, duplicated or transmitted without direct written permission from the author or the publisher. Under no circumstances will any blame or legal responsibility be held against the publisher, or author, for any damages, reparation, or monetary loss due to the information contained within this book. Either directly or indirectly.

Legal Notice: This book is copyright protected. This book is only for personal use. You cannot amend, distribute, sell, use, quote or paraphrase any part, or the content within this book, without the consent of the author or publisher.

Disclaimer Notice: Please note the information contained within this document is for educational and entertainment purposes only. All effort has been executed to present accurate, up to date, and reliable, complete information. No warranties of any kind are declared or implied. Readers acknowledge that the author is not engaging in the rendering of legal, financial, medical or professional advice. The content within this book has been derived from various sources. Please consult a licensed professional before attempting any techniques outlined in this book.

By reading this document, the reader agrees that under no circumstances is the author responsible for any losses, direct or indirect, which are incurred as a result of the use of information contained within this document, including, but not limited to, errors, omissions, or inaccuracies.

TABLE OF CONTENTS

INTRODUCTION 3

CAPITOL 1 DEFENDING YOURSELF AGAINST MANIPULATION 5

    WHAT YOU NEED TO DO TO OVERCOME MANIPULATION 5
    HOW TO CONFRONT A BULLY SAFELY 22
    YOUR INFLUENCE SKILL SET 22
    WHAT TO DO IN CASE OF MANIPULATION? 27

CHAPTER 12: PROTECTING YOURSELF FROM MANIPULATION .. 31

    STRATEGIES FOR PROTECTION AGAINST MANIPULATION 31

CONCLUSION 56

Introduction

Every aspect of human life has two sides-positive and negative, but it depends on the human how he or she utilizes it for their good as well as for others. Consider manipulation as a part of dark psychology, and it is used greatly for the wrongdoings and harmful deeds. On the other hand, it can be utilized positively as well, but it's all in your hand how you want to utilize it. As far as persuasion is concerned, people use it in every field and part of life. For example, a salesman will always try to persuade you to buy his or her recommended product even if you do not want to. Persuasion also has two aspects of being applied. If you try to persuade a person to do something illegal or unethical, that is part of dark psychology but if you persuade someone to get out or leave a certain thing that is not beneficial in any means, let's say suicide, then you are using it for the purpose of good. Everything you do or perceive is totally in the human mind, and you are the controller of it. If you don't want to, then no one can make you do things without your will and consent. Also, it is an essential part of living life to observe your surroundings and the people who are around you. If you do not notice the small things and interpret them wisely, then you are more likely to fall prey for something negative and hazardous. Facial expressions, body language, gestures, and the words and tone used, can predict a lot about people if observed closely. If you fail to recognize such signals that are inclined towards negativity, then you will be unable to keep yourself safe from them. Dark psychology is considered to start from the point where you have no intent or motive to do things except for your self-satisfaction and pleasure, and in return, it is damaging to the other person or even the community. Every living individual has this dark side, but not all of them let that side overcome them. Once you are exposed to that side, there is no coming back. So always watch yourself and your surroundings so that you can keep yourself off of any harm. Persuasion, manipulation, and other forms of influence are ubiquitous. You can pick up on some obvious signs here and there, but there are also hidden secret ways that others control you which you might never be able to fully comprehend.

To those who aren't fully aware of manipulation and what it is all about, it is hard to see that this process takes up three steps. Most of us will just think of manipulation as one thing—there needs to be two things in addition to the act of manipulation, which will make sure that the manipulation is successful. Perhaps you are trying to sell something, maybe yourself or your brand, and you need to figure out how to get people to be more persuaded by you to help you achieve the things that you want in this life. No matter where you are or what you are trying to do, you have all the tools that you will ever need to be persuasive or influential with you already.

Before getting into this book, there are a few things that you need to know to be introduced to this topicto get into the right mindset as you read through this text. First, understand that there are no two manipulators that are alike. There are no two easily persuaded people that are the same either. Though it might seem like this sometimes, especially since you can influence a group all at once, you can't let yourself fall into a thinking pattern where you place everyone in the same category.

Don't blame yourself for not being aware of the ways that you have been manipulated in the past. Regret isn't going to do you any good in this journey, so it's best to leave those feelings of, "I wish I would have known this sooner," behind. All that you can do now is move forward, and we will help you every step of the way!

CAPITOL 1
Defending Yourself Against Manipulation

WHAT YOU NEED TO DO TO OVERCOME MANIPULATION

We have come to a point where we are here to talk about the basic skills to overcome manipulation. Moreover, manipulation will only work if you allow them to control you. Much like hypnosis, any hypnosis is self-hypnosis. What we are trying to state here is that knowledge that you are being manipulated defeats its entire purpose.

ESTABLISH A CLEAR SENSE OF SELF

There is a need to know your identity, what your needs and wants are, what your emotions are, and what you are fond of and not fond of. You must learn to accept these and not become apologetic, as these are the things that make you, you. At times, we dread that in the event of speaking up, we are viewed by others as egotistical and called out for being selfish. Nevertheless, knowing your identity or what you need in life is not at all an act of selfishness. Self-centeredness is demanding that you always get what you want or that others have always put your needs and wants first. Similarly, when another person calls you out for not following their orders or fulfilling their needs and wants, they are the ones being selfish, not you.

SAY "NO" DESPITE THE OTHER PERSON'S DISAPPROVAL

The ability to say "no" despite somebody's objection is a solid demonstration. Individuals who can do this are present in reality. Because in reality, there is no way that we can accommodate all of their needs and wants. When this happens, they will become baffled, even disappointed. However, keep in mind that what they are feeling is part of human nature. Most of these individuals would then forgive and forget. Sound individuals realize that getting what you want all the time is not possible, even when the desires are genuine. In any case, when we cannot endure another person's mistake or objection, it ends up hard stating "no." It winds up more diligently for us to state it or have limits. Manipulators exploit this shortcoming and use dissatisfaction and objection in extraordinary structures to get us to do what they need.

TOLERATE THE OTHER PERSON'S NEGATIVE AFFECT

We can demonstrate compassion for people's pity, hurt, or even annoyance when accommodating them without needing to back down and reverse our decision. Keep in mind, a solid relationship is described by common minding, shared genuineness, and shared regard. If you are involved with somebody who uses manipulation and unhealthy control consistently, begin to see little propensities that may not be clear to you at first.

KEEP A CONVERSATIONS JOURNAL

There are usually some kinds of signs that send hints that somebody is trying to manipulate them. Those aren't always easy to find, of course, unless you've been in the situation before or recognize coercion. One strategy that you can do if you feel you are being manipulated by someone is to keep a journal of what's said. You can write down your conversations or stuff they say to you randomly. You should even write down what they are doing at the same time. Although this may sound like an unusual thing to do, it will help you understand what is happening, since manipulators are operating on an emotional level. This is sometimes hard to notice, especially if you are already lacking in self-confidence. You may also include how the mentioned circumstance or words made you feel. You may find a connection between what is stated by the manipulator and how you feel. You might find, for example, that your self-image is starting to diminish. When you notice this, it is a sign that you have to stay away from the person or get out of the relationship as quickly as possible.

CONFRONTING MANIPULATORS ABOUT THEIR CONDUCT

With some people, that will be easier than others. For example, if your supervisor is the manipulator, and you need your job, you may not be able to confront them directly. You might also have a hard time confronting your significant other, especially if they've lowered your self-esteem. Confronting the manipulator, however, is a perfect way to let them know you understand their actions and you won't stand for it. When you are following this path, you want to be aware of the other tactics that they may be used against you. They might try to create a distraction, for example, or try to play the victim. They might also blame someone else for their behavior or tell you that you imagined it all. You need to be firm when confronting a manipulator. You need to be fully persuaded and understand that they will try and exploit you because they don't want other people to catch on to their actions. You also need to be careful, as some manipulators can become passive-aggressive or violent.

PUT THE FOCUS OF THE MANIPULATORS

You can also focus on the manipulator, in addition to confronting them. You can do this by asking a range of questions regarding their motive. You want to try and find out why they act the way they do, which is the foundation of dark psychology. Some of the questions you may ask are: "Do you feel reasonable?" "What will I get out of this?" "Is this helpful?" "That's what you want from me (state their request)." You show the manipulator what they are doing by asking questions like these. They would be remorseful or alter their request if they are not a master manipulator and did not intend to take part in that action. If they're a master manipulator, however, they'll think of other tactics to turn it back on you. They will try to act like the victim, by asking "Why are you attacking me? "or by saying "I'm just trying to help; I don't appreciate being attacked like this."

START DRIVING YOUR AGENDA

Manipulators don't want to win over other people. This puts them in a threatened position. The more you succeed, though, the more you drive a manipulator backward. Your ability to believe in and continue to succeed in yourself will depend on how long you know the manipulator and how close you are to them. For example, if you have been emotionally beaten down by the manipulator, it will be much harder to remain motivated and work hard to succeed. If you've just met them, without too much trouble you'll be able to continue pushing towards your success. Of course, having the mindset of believing that you can fulfill your dreams, and supporting people will help eliminate the manipulator through your success. And if you need to speak to someone to get better mentally and emotionally, this is what you do.

DON'T GET PHYSICALLY TIED UP

While sometimes we get trapped by a manipulator because we don't know their personality, other times we know they're manipulators, but they still need to keep in touch because they're colleagues or family. You need to protect yourself in a different way when this is the situation because you cannot simply ignore them. A lot of people also recommend you do your best not to get emotionally attached. For some people, this will be tougher than others. If you're a more emotional person, you'll be struggling to avoid becoming emotionally attached as your relationships are emotionally based.

One way to do this is to ensure that they know the boundaries. You'll also need to make sure that you stick to your limits. If you cross your boundaries, manipulators don't care, so you need to protect yourself. Tell them if you think they're jumping a fence. Don't fall back for any of their techniques and don't turn back.

DON'T FEED THE DRAMA

One of the most essential things a manipulator thrives on is suspense. For this reason, they often disagree with someone or something that will cause people to respond. So one of the best ways to stop a manipulator in their tracks is to tell them "you are right." Manipulators aren't used to having people to agree with them, and when you do, they'll be left speechless. This also creates a threat that could make them want to leave you alone. They may feel that they can't trap you with their techniques, especially if you do so right away. This is not to say that they will not try. Manipulators also aim to bring people into the network. Letting them win the argument, even if it upsets your ego a little bit, is much better than falling victim to their pitfalls.

HAVE A HEALTHY ATTITUDE

Having a healthy mindset is another way of eliminating a manipulator from your life. You want to make sure you feel confident that you can stop them from using techniques against you. You will want to make sure you feel good about your self-esteem and self-image. At the same time, you want to understand how they manipulate you. To battle them, you need to have a grasp on their techniques. You have to understand they probably won't stop with just one technique. More than likely they will use a few in hopes they can start breaking you down. The stronger you remain, the more likely the manipulator will leave you alone. If you always push them away, call them out on their behavior, and continue to believe in yourself, manipulators won't spend a lot of time trying to use different techniques.

MEDITATION

Many people don't realize how helpful meditation can be. Meditation is not just about keeping you relaxed but also about keeping you optimistic and feeling good about yourself. When you feel this way, it's easier to remove the negativity from your life, which means manipulators. Meditation is easy, so you don't have to put too much time aside. You can schedule meditation in around ten minutes out of your day. Find a time and place where you can be on your own and without interruption. You also want to keep it quiet, so you can concentrate on eliminating your body and mind from the negativity. Many people would be using relaxation exercises to help them remain focused when meditating. This is when you close your eyes and start to breathe normally. You want to concentrate on the breaths. Notice the feeling of your body on your clothes or put one hand on your chest and the other on your stomach. Feel how your hands move in and out as you breathe. Then you focus on deep breaths. Take a deep breath in, then slowly exhale. Finish the exercise until you feel soothed.

In addition to helping you eliminate manipulators who have not become a close person in your life, meditation will also help you manage your life with a manipulator. Of course, if your significant other is a manipulator for your mental health and safety, you want to leave but meditation can help give you strength. It will give you the strength to concentrate on your attitude and find ways to defend yourself against the tactics of coercion. It may give you the strength to leave as well, once you're ready.

ASEPSIS AND TOTAL AVOIDANCE

That is, do not get close to a handler, to avoid contact and contagion as much as possible. Of all the strategies, this is the most effective. It's not the most epic, but it does work the best. The first security strategy in any situation is always avoidance. The basic strategy for winning a battle with a manipulator is not to enter the battle. That is the only correct maneuver because any other way has consequences.

"A manipulator is an expert in fighting in the mud, from behind, and with low blows, he will win against us if we go down to his ground."

In bad times, both personal and business, there is a temptation to listen to more dubious clients, frequently worse companies, fall into "get rich effortlessly" or "it's always someone else's fault" schemes (so better end with them). We have to avoid that as much as possible; we have to leave them alone and put a bell of silence on the manipulator.

It is far better to miss an "opportunity" to work with a manipulator than to get bogged down with one. Nobody goes around exposing themselves to the flu just to show how strong they are. Our primary strategy with disease and with manipulation should be the same: do not enter their radius of action as far as possible.

CUT THE ROPE AT ONCE, AS SOON AS POSSIBLE

The former is the best strategy, but it is impossible to avoid 100% manipulation. Sometimes they will catch us off guard and, at other times, circumstances will drag us into a situation, whether we like it or not. There will also be times when it will be friends, family, or acquaintances who will be in a manipulative situation and we will have to get involved to help them.

"In these circumstances, and from experience, the appropriate strategy is to cut ties with the manipulator as soon as possible. We will do it quickly as if it were a clean blow of the sword. Then we take as much distance as possible."

I know it may seem suggestive to be the vigilante and believe that we will not be fooled but resist the temptation. Every minute that you spend with a manipulator, you will be draining precious energy. If we are there, the strategy is to disengage from the fight as soon as possible, "hit" only to gain distance, and then avoid further contact in the future.

If you are involved in business with a manipulator, terminate any contracts, say no to the slightest bit that you propose, seek outside support, and do not isolate yourself by listening only to the manipulator.

NEVER DIRECTLY CONFRONT A MANIPULATOR IF YOU CAN AVOID IT

If he does, he will flee by other roads, mount the number, play the victim, or use one of his hat's many tricks. We have to be smarter than them.

"If you spot a manipulator, don't go straight for it, look for an indirect angle, and strike with one of the following strategies to break away from their influence and distance yourself."

I repeat, do not go to direct war.

NEVER, NEVER, LOSE YOUR TEMPER

As the Americans say: "Business is business. "This phrase alludes to a philosophy whereby there is no reason for the emotional to get in the way of business. With that mentality of separating the professional from the personal, many businesses take some huge (business) stab wounds and solve them with, "It's just business."

"The exercise to be learned is that, in business and against manipulation, you never lose your temper."

If emotion surfaces, the manipulator wins. If he fails, he begins to despair, uses more violent tactics, exposes himself, makes mistakes, discovers his game, and loses the ability to manipulate.

The manipulator seeks the brawl, and if the other loses the papers, we have to turn it around and use that strategy against him. We must know that we are winning every second that we do not lose our temper and do not get carried away by emotion.

Never get upset by a manipulator, be it in a personal or professional situation. Let's see the situation for what it is, a surgical operation to remove it from our environment, and not do more damage. It will twist, scream, and kick, getting louder and dirtier, like when little children get angry. But if we hold the guy, he loses.

LEARN TO INTERPRET THE SIGNALS.

It is vital to recognize a manipulator and be aware of our emotional state in a negotiation, sale, or discussion with one.

The four main clues that should set off the alarms because we are in front of a professional liar are:

INSULATION

Trying to isolate ourselves in a conversation, a situation, or something that we do not consult or talk about with others, are signs of manipulation. Isolation is a typical manipulative tactic that is imperative, such as for cults, to make them work. Any sensible person who proposes something to us has no problem in consulting other opinions.

RUSH AND PRESSURE

When someone tries to get us to rashly buy a product, sign a contract, make any decision, or go out of business, something stinks. You have to distance yourself, consult other options, and decide calmly. "We should never make an important decision in a hurry or an upset, emotional state."

EXCESS OF EMOTIONS

Be careful when an excess of emotionality is used in the speeches, they make us or the situations they put us in, easier to manipulate. I have seen firsthand how certain unethical companies in the field of self-help act, for example. They organize weekends where attendees are isolated in a hotel or spa; they are put in an altered and highly elevated emotional state (with exercises, practices, and speeches that strike a chord). Then all this is used to sell more expensive programs and courses, of course, in a rush and pressure using a false shortage (another typical manipulation trick). "If you can put someone in a sufficiently upset emotional state, you can make them believe what you want."

EXCESS "LOVE" AND ATTENTION

One of the cults' preferred strategies for attracting followers is called the "love bomb." It is characterized because everyone accepts you unconditionally, smiles at you, and behaves like the best thing that ever happened to them, even though they hardly know you. There is no criticism; no one says no to anything, it's all gestures and acceptance smiles.

Acceptance is a harsh drug for anyone, but especially for those who have barely been able to obtain it, such as the lonely, the marginalized, or those going through a hard time. Those can all be us, and those are the scapegoats. We can all fall into the "love bomb." Likewise, the lack of seriousness, the excess confidence, the refusal to sign contracts or agreements because everyone here "are friends"... All of these are usually signs of manipulation.

IF IN DOUBT, ALSO SAY THAT YOU WANT TO GET A SECOND OPINION TO SEE THE MANIPULATOR'S REACTION.

Similar to the previous time strategy, in this case, we say we want a second opinion. Even when we are responsible for the decision to be made, we can always say that we must consult someone else: a lawyer, our spouse, a friend who is an expert on the subject.

It is about trying to get out of the isolation trap with arguments that are difficult to refute. A desperate effort on the other not to consult a superior or an expert is a sign that we are possibly being manipulated. These two strategies work as a detector for manipulators and differentiate them directly in a delicate situation.

DO NOT GIVE IN TO A MANIPULATOR OR IN THE MOST INOFFENSIVE DETAILS

If you think you are dealing with a manipulator, don't say yes to anything. No matter how innocent he seems. If we do, we are at risk of using cognitive dissonance (one of the fundamental principles of persuasion) to make us take a seemingly simple step and then gradually get more agreement from our part. When we realize it, it has pushed us to the bottom of the web.

If you know you are involved with a manipulator, never get closer than necessary, never say yes and never think you have everything under control. It must be noted that often and we are not obliged to justify this refusal, we are within our rights, and "no" is a complete sentence.

If he insists, we say the same, "no"; we do not add additional excuses that he can grab on to. Manipulators are adept at emotional blackmail and trying to get excuses to see how to turn them around.

BE VERY CLEAR ABOUT THE INITIAL OBJECTIVE YOU HAVE IN MIND

This is the first golden rule of negotiation, but it should be remembered for any situation in which we interact with a manipulator.

"If your objective in the conversation or negotiation with a manipulator is vague and diffused, you will end up at a point that the manipulator wants."

Be very clear about what you want. Never confront a manipulator without knowing precisely what you want to get out of the interaction. If you will cut the ties with the manipulator, focus everything on reducing the links and not moving from there. If you want to hear what he has to say and then reflect ahead of time, with other opinions and without pressure, keep that in mind and don't allow anything else to happen.

Listen to him, and don't let the manipulator get to anything other than the goal you have in mind. Since this is the real world, you should have an ideal target in mind and then a realistic goal, being prepared to compromise (though not quickly) from that ideal goal to the actual one. However, that is the minimum limit, do not give another step.

Know your destiny, as far as you can give in, and then be like Ulysses returning from Troy. Hold on tight to your targets and resist any manipulative siren calls.

NEVER USE THE SAME WEAPONS AS A MANIPULATOR

There is a powerful temptation to use weapons of manipulation against the manipulator. To respond with fallacies, try to isolate him, do emotional blackmail, or put on an act ourselves to increase that emotion in the situation. "Don't fall for it, because they are based on lies, which has practical consequences. I do not want to sound like a preacher, but they never come out for free."

There is a red line that delimits persuasion, and on the other side are manipulation techniques. The first few times, this line commands respect, and it is difficult to cross it. But when we've crossed it the first time and have fallen into unethical manipulation, the line is blurred even for a legitimate purpose. That way, it is much easier to transfer it again a second time.

Do it a few more times, and the line will be erased, and we will have become one of them.

But it is also that manipulation is not necessary. There is a large amount of material on ethical persuasion to learn; you can use scarcity without isolating or pressing; you can use cognitive dissonance without it being a trap to fleece a victim. Always remember to have ethics, because if there is one thing I have learned, it is that manipulators do not end up well.

ACT QUICKLY

It's great that you have come to terms with the reality of things, but defense against these dark manipulative tactics entail so much more. Attempting to defend yourself from the claws of these manipulators, is often intense and exhilarating at first.

This intensity of these emotions may cause one to slowly slide into denial. The more you delay in taking any action, that is usually what accelerates the onset of this denial, and when it happens, there are high chances that you might relapse and end up getting trapped in the same web.

This can be avoided by taking action immediately when you realize that someone is trying to manipulate you. This can present itself in the simplest of ways, like when informing a close friend of the reality of a particular situation may be all that's needed so set in motion a series of events that will eventually lead to your freedom.

You should know that the fabric of illusion is made from a tougher material than glass after choosing to act. The illusion could work its way back into your heart with your emotions in high gear by using fragments of your emotions to fix it.

When a liar is caught in a lie, he or she may attempt to recruit others to enforce that lie when they feel that they are no longer holding you.

A deceptive partner with whom you have recently broken things off, would at this point try to use the other mutual relationships in your life to change your mind.

If you want to get out of this unscathed, you will need both your logic and instincts. Although the truth of the situation is that when you discover that you've been lied to consistently, you become emotionally scarred, so the issue of leaving the situation unscathed becomes unlikely.

Priority should be given, however, to take the route that allows you to leave this toxic situation without harming yourself further. You're all over the place emotionally.

Rage, anger, hurt, and deception is the tip of the iceberg, but logically, you need to think. Keep your head above the water and warn yourself.

TRUST YOUR INSTINCTS

While your brain interprets signals based on facts, logic, and sometimes experience, your heart works in the opposite direction by screening information through an emotional filter. The only thing that picks up vibrations is your gut instinct, which neither the heart nor the brain can pick on.

If you can groom yourself to the point where you recognize your inner voice and are trained to react to it, you will lower your chances of being seduced by people trying to work on you with their manipulative will.

To begin, it's hard to recognize this voice. That's because we allowed voices of doubt, self-discrimination as well as the critics' loud voices within to be heard and without drawing out our authentic voice throughout our lives.

Your survival depends on this voice or instinct. So, trust that when it kicks in, your brain neurons can still process things in your immediate vicinity.

Some people call it intuition, and some refer to it as instinct, especially when it comes to relationships, they are undoubtedly the same thing. You must accept that it may not always make logical sense to start trusting your instincts.

If you've ever been in the middle of doing something and experienced the feeling of being watched all of a sudden, then you know what I mean. You don't have eyes at the back of your head, there's no one else with you in the room, but you get that tiny shiver running down your spine and the "sudden knowledge" that you're being watched. That's what I'm talking about.

The first step to connect with your instinct is to decode your mind with the voices you've let in. With meditation, you can do this. Forget the chatter of "he said, she said." Concentrate on your center. You are the voice you know. Next, be careful about your thoughts. Don't just throw away the eclectic monologue in your head. Rather go with the flow of thoughts.

Why do you think of a certain person in some way? How do you feel so deeply about this person, even if you only know each other for a few days? What's that nagging feeling about this other person that you have? You get more tuned to your intuition as you explore your thoughts and understand when your instincts kick in and how to react to it.

You may need to learn to take a step back to pause and think if you are the kind of person who prefers to make decisions in the spur of the moment.

This moment in which you pause, allows you to reflect on your decisions and evaluate them. The next part is hard, and it couldn't be followed by many people. Unfortunately, you can't skip or navigate around this step.

This part has to do with trust. You need to be open to the idea of trusting yourself and trusting others to be able to trust your instinct. Your failure to trust others would just make you paranoid, and it's not your instincts that kick in when you're paranoid.

It's the fear in you. Fear tends to turn every molehill into a mountain. You must let go of your fear, embrace confidence, and let that lead in your new relationships.

You are better able to hear the voice inside without the roadblocks put up by fear in your mind. Finally, your priorities need to be reevaluated.

If your mind is at the forefront of money and material possessions, you may not be able to see the past. Any interaction you have with people would be interpreted as people trying to take advantage of you, and if you dwell on that frequently enough, it will soon become your reality.

You attract into your life what you think of. If you're constantly thinking about material wealth, you're only going to attract people who think like you. Using this as a guide, look at all your relationships with this new hindsight; the old, the new, and the prospective.

Don't enter a relationship that expects to be played. Be open when you approach them, whether it's a business relationship, a romantic relationship, or even a regular acquaintance. You can get the right feedback about them from your intuition.

Do not step into this thinking, too, that your gut will tell you to run in the opposite direction when you meet suspect people.

How to Confront a Bully Safely

Not all manipulators resort to bullying, but many of them do. Someone is being a bully when they use intimidation or harm to get what they want from you. Always remember, that a bully chooses people they see as weak to pick on, and compliance and passivity will only strengthen this. However, a lot of bullies are afraid and insecure deep down, so when their victim starts to stand up for themselves, this will often lead the bully to back off. Whether this situation is occurring in a playground or at the office, it applies, most of the time. Keep in mind that many bullies have withstood bullying and violence. Although this doesn't excuse their behaviors, it does help the victim to understand.

Your Influence Skill Set

Clarity of Purpose

An important facet of the ability to influence others is your clarity. Know what you want and have a clear plan of how you will get it. Whether you're working in sales and trying to improve the team's quarterly figures or trying to encourage a student to be more diligent with study, or to set them on a career path – know what the objective is. The only way you can succeed in influencing someone to behave in a desired way is if you are clear about what you hope to achieve. You don't get in your car to drive to a destination you've never been without setting the GPS. The same goes for the application of influence toward achieving a desired effect or goal. Know where you're going.

Always be prepared in advance, with the following:

A list of prioritized objectives.

A clear picture of the final destination (what it looks like).

Preparing the environment.

If you are seeking to reach an agreement with someone, you need to make them feel comfortable. You also need to be relaxed and yourself. At the same time, for effective communication (which is important when you want to influence someone's behavior, as this book is explaining) you need to make the environment conducive to your interaction. You need to have in place a planned sequence of events at that meeting beforehand.

The best way to achieve this is to draw up a meeting agenda and circulate it to those who will attend, one day before the meeting. In this way, everyone knows what to expect and what shape the meeting will take. The agenda should make clear what the goals of the meeting are. Checking off the items on it should move you closer to the agreement, if not enable all present to reach consensus to move forward. The logical sequence of events represented by following an agenda is a function of a critically structured plan. Having a plan of such quality never fails to impress.

CONSENSUS BUILDING

In building consensus, you're making it clear you are open to suggestions (which you should always be, regardless of your single-minded focus on your ultimate goal). Hearing what people say and truly listening means you're not planning a response while they're talking. It means you're actively hearing everything they say. Subtext, word choice, and tone are all important and so are your skills at hearing what's being said. Proceeding with these skills in play can provide you with the basis for genuine and not false consensus.

False consensus is reached when people are "heard out", but not "heard". These are two entirely different animals. The first is the condescending indulgence of hearing what no longer matters because a decision has already been made and the results of that decision, imposed. Being heard means that influence on the final decision is still a possibility and that what's offered may result in concessions, if it features actual merit.

Being present to the input of others and being able to integrate their thoughts and suggestions into an existing plan is a function of leadership. Leadership is not imposed. Leadership is extended to others as a service. Consensus building is a way to bring forward the knowledge of the team and add it to your own. In the case of reaching an agreement, it's the foundation of lasting relationships that won't later be ruptured by objections to not being heard. This is extremely important. Autocratic leadership is unwelcome and will not survive for long. It is a corrosive leadership style that is not sustainable.

CREATING RAPPORT

When someone begins to enjoy your company, it becomes much easier for you to enlist their support. This makes it more likely they'll support your viewpoint in situations in which it counts. Allies are people who like and trust you. Your relationships are what will move your goals forward and create a foundation for your success and that of your allies. People, while perhaps not being entirely aware of this on an intellectual level, know this instinctively. That is why you must prioritize establishing rapport with others. It's the basis of strong allegiances.

Part of creating rapport is establishing the common interests you hold with others. Taking an interest in them and offering them information about who you are is how this is achieved. Being too veiled about yourself makes you appear cold, calculating, and detached. Establish that you're open and also, a person who can be trusted.

It's also important to establish easily with others and one way this can be done is to mirror the body language. You'll probably find (if you pay attention), that you do this anyway when you've begun to establish rapport with someone. Mirroring body language sends the unconscious signal that there is a bond already established between two people and that they're on the same team. Mirroring speech patterns is another way of doing this. Repeating keywords with enthusiasm at opportune times is another natural way we tell each other we're enjoying a conversation or agreeing with each other. Nod, smile, and respond positively when you sense a common theme emerging in conversation. This sends the message that you're accessible on the most basic, human level.

SUGGESTIONS INSTEAD OF DEMANDS

People routinely bridle at directives. In Western societies where individualism is a way of life, we like to believe in our autonomy as a value. That means it's not the best course of action to demand things from people. Much more effective is suggesting a course of action and building consensus based on the suggestion while being open to input and concessions to other points of view. This is the democratic way of achieving goals and one that is completely manageable with the application of a deft hand.

Here are examples of language that gives your listener the option to chip in and yet still leaves you the "wiggle room" to get to where you believe you need to go:

"Would you be interested in doing a-b-c?"

"Could you be interested in doing a-b-c?"

"I think we should do a-b-c. What do you think?"

"Do you think this is the best way forward, or do you have other ideas?"

Leaving space for opinion and input, while still advancing the validity of your own opinion is the stuff of which influence is made. While you're providing people with a rationale for your point of view, your willingness to entertain amendments to that point of view only increases your influential power. Imposition rarely ends in anything but resentment. By building consensus through input and exchange, you will still arrive at the goal you have in mind, but you'll do it with the support of a willing team, signed on to the plan in question. A fringe benefit? That input will undoubtedly improve on the original plan and will result in satisfaction on the part of all involved.

HEIGHTENING YOUR AWARENESS

Awareness of the responses of other people to what you're saying is key to influential action. What are their facial expressions telling you? Their body language and word choices? What about tone and pitch? All these factors are rich with information that you can draw on to temper your pitch and get people on your side. It can also cue you to back off and change lanes, while you re-group and allow others their input.

Active listening, while employing body language (head nodding, eye contact) and assenting noises ("uh-huh", "yes", "I see") is also about deeply engaging with what's being said and the complimentary messages being sent by the speaker. Your awareness in crucial situations, of all the factors that create a communicative environment, is of the utmost importance. You need to be aware, not only of what's being said but implications about what's intended, what's not being said, and the speaker's frame of mind. All these factors work together to form a more concise body of information from which you may draw to apply influential action.

WHAT TO DO IN CASE OF MANIPULATION?

You must also be aware that the manipulator will never change because he does not do it for a specific logical reason that has a right place in real life. He does it because he needs it and this need is dictated by his personality, along with his dark and problematic psychological state; in practice if he does it today then tomorrow he will start looking for reasons to go back to doing it again and again and again and again.

For this reason, a good way to escape manipulation is to remove the manipulator, be it a partner or an employer, a neighbor, or an acquaintance. When this is not possible because there is coexistence with this individual, then we must defend ourselves and a good way to do this is to be aware, as I said before, of the way the manipulator operates and to establish a virtual border between the manipulator and manipulated so that the latter does not feel responsible for all the problems that arise from this "coexistence". In other words, you have to ignore it!

To defend yourself from manipulation you also need to be able to recognize and manage your emotions and your body to understand and accept when you are being manipulated and the traumas that have been suffered. To practice advice on how to defend yourself from manipulation, you must first be able to accept it. Dark manipulation is defined so, primarily, because it is a weapon generally used by psychologically problematic subjects and believe me you can meet one more frequently than you can imagine. Secondly, it is called so because it is manipulation that has purposes that are not enough to be defined as negatives as they are subtle.

HOW TO AVOID BEING NEGATIVELY MANIPULATED BY OTHERS

Be aware of your rights: The absolute most important rule you can follow when dealing with someone who wants to manipulate you in negative ways, is to know your worth and rights. This way, you will always know when someone is attempting to violate them. So long as others are not getting harmed in the process, you should be defending yourself. Every human should have the right to have differing opinions from others, to protect yourself, to say "no" when you need to, and to decide what's important to you. You should also have the right of expressing your wants, opinions, and feelings, and always be treated with respect.

Unfortunately, the world has plenty of people who won't want to acknowledge or respect your rights, especially negative manipulators. You will also come into contact with others who generally wish to take advantage of any opportunity. However, you can proudly defy this by letting them know that you are the one who runs your life, no one else.

Maintain healthy distance: Another way to tell who is manipulative, is to pay attention to the way someone acts in varying situations and in front of various individuals. Although everyone, to a degree, puts on different faces depending on where they are, most people who are harmfully manipulative are extreme about it. They might, for example, be extremely polite and friendly to one person, and completely disrespect another, or act like a victim one second, and then act controlling immediately after.

If you notice someone acting this way regularly, it's a good sign to distance yourself from them and not engage with them unless it's an absolute necessity. Usually, the reasons behind these types of behavior are complicated, and it isn't your duty or responsibility to help or change that person. Trying to do so will often only lead to suffering on your part, so it's better not to expect much when you notice these signs.

Don't blame yourself: A person who wishes to manipulate others in harmful ways searches for weaknesses to exploit, so it makes sense that someone who has been victimized by one might blame themselves or feel inadequate. But in a situation like this, you should remember that it isn't you that's the issue here; you are being pressured to feel bad by someone else who is very good at making people feel bad.

This is how they get their way. Instead, think about the relationship you have with this person and ask yourself if they are respecting you, demanding reasonable things from you, and whether you are both benefiting, or only one of you is. Ask yourself, also, if you feel good about yourself after spending time with this person, or if you would feel better being around them less. The way you answer these questions will lead to important answers about where the issue lies in the situation.

Questioning them: Eventually, this type of person will demand or request things from you. Many times, these requests or others will consider their needs, while completely ignoring yours. Next time you receive a solicitation that is completely unreasonable, turn the focus back to them by asking some questions. Ask them if their request is reasonable, or if what they are asking from you is fair. You can also try asking if you get to have an opinion in this matter or ask what benefit you will be gaining from the arrangement.

Each time you ask questions like this, you are holding a mirror up to them, allowing them to see what they are truly asking of you. If they are self-aware, they will likely retract their request or demand. But there may be some cases, such as dealing with a narcissist, who will keep insisting without even considering your questions. If that happens, follow these guidelines.

Don't answer Immediately: One way to combat manipulation is to use time as a resource. Often, the manipulator will not only ask you to fulfill an unreasonable demand, but they will want an answer immediately. When this happens, rather than answering right away, use time and distance yourself from their request and influence. This can be done by telling them that you will think about it. Although these words are simple, they give your power back to you, giving you the option to weigh the advantages and disadvantages of the situation and let you work out something better, if need be.

Teach yourself to say "no" when needed: Saying "no" is difficult for many people, since we are often taught and conditioned to be polite whenever possible. Being able to confidently but politely say "no" comes with learning communication skills. When this is articulated effectively, you can hold onto your self-respect, and also continue a healthy relationship. Keep in mind that your rights include deciding what matters to you, being able to turn down a request free from guilt and choosing health and happiness for yourself. You are responsible for your life, not the person who is making unreasonable demands of you.

Create a consequence: Next time a negative manipulator tries to violate your rights, and refuses to accept your answer, set a consequence for their behavior. Knowing how to assert and identify appropriate consequences is a crucial skill for standing down someone who is being very difficult or disrespectful. If you can articulate this clearly and thoroughly, your consequences will cause them to pause and stop violating you, shifting to a position of respect.

Chapter 12:

Protecting Yourself From Manipulation

STRATEGIES FOR PROTECTION AGAINST MANIPULATION

We all love pursuing the other sex every now and then- both men and women. It's fun and a good sport, as long as we're frank about it and bear in mind that it's all about passion. Why? For what? Since it's deceit to try and love cannot be exploited-we don't find love; love finds us. So, we should view a relationship of love as sacred ground.

Sadly, many people believe in deception – both in relationships and in industry. In my early twenties, I read something that stuck for good in my subconsciousness: if you can align yourself with the universe, it's easy to achieve success. What does this mean for this topic? It means manipulations are pointless at the end of the day. Manipulations may potentially offer a short-term benefit, but in the long run, it will eventually lead to consequences as they are opposed by the universe. But if we go with the celestial wind, we'll gravitate toward our target – more or less effortlessly. Too good to be real? Every one of us is playing a part in the cosmic game. In the grand scheme of things, we just have to know our position and let it play out. And Jesus said his cross is as light as a feather. Of course, this means giving up several wishes and aspirations that aren't part of our cameo. However, our celestial intent typically turns out to be much more grandiose than our puny, selfish ambitions.

That being said, we also need to defend ourselves from other people's childish manipulations, including those around us. Don't take this lightly; it's painful, emotional coercion and can leave deep wounds on people's psyche and soul. Once you are in a state of exploitation, it is very difficult to get out. But don't take this affair too seriously, we're doing a lot of things subconsciously, and your partner may not even know that she's manipulating you.

There will always be people trying to shake your trust - people trying to instill seeds of self-doubt inside you. Such people would do their utmost to trick you into thinking that their beliefs are objective facts. They're trying to tell you everyone in the world thinks you're rude, nuts, or not nice. Then they'll tell you how much they're worried about you, how you're living your life, spending your money, raising your children, on and on.

If you don't change the way they want you to change, then your life will be destroyed. This is what they want to believe. The truth isyou don't want to help these people. They want to get you under control. We want you to adjust, not to make your life easier, but to affirm their lives and prevent you from overgrowing them.

DON'T GET ANGRY

Manipulative people are not preoccupied with your needs. They worry about their interests. Once you allow manipulative people in your life, it can be extremely difficult to get rid of them. The trick is to have enough self-control to send the boot to dishonest people as soon as you see them. Here are a few ways to get rid of manipulative people from your life:

LISTEN TO YOUR EMOTIONS

when something is wrong, the body sends translatable signals into a sense of general malaise. It is always good to listen to these subliminal messages and try to understand what's wrong.

CHANGE YOUR POINT OF VIEW

If you happen to be in a situation where you feel the stench of manipulation, pretend to be a third person who "observes from outside" what is happening. This is because often we get involved in feelings and we don't judge things for what they are. By following this advice, you can give an objective assessment of the situation.

MAKE IT A REASON

This is easy to understand. You have to understand that manipulation is part of life, such as luck or the sun rising in the morning and setting in the evening. It is something that exists and for which you cannot do anything. On the contrary, you can try to improve and develop your positive side, this will help you a lot.

As for the tactics to be used to defend against a manipulator, having unmasked it, we can say that it will be useful to follow one or more of those listed below:

EXPRESS WHAT YOU DISAGREE WITH

This is because the manipulator criticizes everything, or almost everything, and consequently the victim tries to defend himself in every way to deny it, becoming more and more aggressive (in this case he falls completely into the trap). In this case, the victim only has to express his point of view clearly, calmly, and simply to make the manipulator understand that whatever he says, he will not be able to change his opinion in the least. This will strongly destabilize the manipulator.

ALWAYS SPEAK IN THE FIRST PERSON

Following this simple advice and pretending that the manipulator does the same is important. Many times, the manipulator speaks in third person and remains very vague in expressing his concepts and attacking someone. They never do it directly. This is because his game is to put others in a bad light so that they cannot be accused, because they don't want to "get their hands dirty".

So if you put your back against the wall with phrases like "what do you think of this person" or "what is your opinion on this situation", you are obliged to express yourself directly and take responsibility for it and maybe, feeling "hunted" will make the manipulator take a step back in their path of manipulation.

ACCEPT YOUR MISTAKES

It seems strange but actually, it is an excellent defense strategy, as the manipulator often focuses on feelings of guilt. They do so by trying to steal the victim's secrets, simple facts, or events, even if they are not necessarily serious, and makes sure that they turn against him making her "feel guilty". This applies both to things that happened in the past, to things that happen in the present, and also to things that could happen in the future.

One strategy to annihilate this type of manipulation is to be able to recognize our mistakes if there have been any. At the same time, we should be able to outline our responsibilities, because if it is true that we have made mistakes, it is also true that we cannot take the blame for everything forever. For example, if a person blames us for our wrong behavior, we can respond by saying sentences like "yes, I made this mistake, but what you say does not concern me", in this case we assume our responsibilities but at the same time we make it clear that in addition to this we are not available to submit to anything else, which makes us appear mature and consequently, not easily manipulated.

SPEAK CALMLY

As mentioned several times in this book, the manipulator prefers emotionally fragile people because he loves to attack the victim's emotions and does not care at all about having a constructive dialogue. By virtue of this, the mistake that many make is that of counterattacking the provocations of the manipulator, which for clarity, is a normal instinctive reaction but in these cases, it is not the right one as he will continue to argue against the victim. It seems absurd but the manipulator is very capable of doing all this. In this case, the defense strategy to be adopted is extremely simple, one only has to recognize that his criticisms are right, never contradict him, and at the same time one must take the right distances in this regard. In practice we can say that you have to make fun of it a bit, using phrases like "I understand your point of view, but I think it's better than ..."
A trick that can help you can replace the term "but" with words like "despite", "nevertheless" "anyway" which according to NLP scholars, would have a "sweeter" but still effective impact.

STRONGLY DENY

When we are confident that what we say is true and we are emotionally strong people, we can also take a more impervious path to defend ourselves from a manipulator and we can deny what he is proposing to us. A dry and firm NO without the use of banal and twisted explanations, perhaps accompanied by an authoritarian body language, will be a good method to desist the manipulator.

Behavioral tone: Having a good behavioral tone is fundamental. It is very similar to a person's emotional intensity, and it is the intensity of one's actions. Don't get the wrong idea because you don't have to scare anyone, it's just about wearing a safe and decisive cover to look like a strong person. If you have or manifest this type of personality, then you will have a good chance that everyone will listen to you because, as the saying goes, actions speak louder than words. This is a good way to be both persuasive and manipulative, so it can also be used as a defense weapon to show the manipulator that you have a strong personality like him and therefore, you are difficult to manipulate.

These tips on how to defend yourself from a manipulator can be applied in multiple cases of manipulation, whether you are dealing with sellers, friends, relatives, employers, people who belong to the religious world, or partners because they are based on the reasoning principles of the manipulator itself and how it works. Keep in mind that manipulative people tend to mask their interests by pretending to help you and then force you to change. It is not to improve your life but so that they can use you, by saying that their opinions, as well as the facts, are the best and yours don't count. They will attract any form of attention and take credit in places where they don't deserve it and will do everything, they canto make sure they keep you from escaping. It is worth noting that once they are established in your life, they are difficult to eliminate. This is why I want to remind you again that the best way to defend yourself from manipulation, as many scholars and authorities in the field say, is to escape from it and the manipulator. You only have to deal with it if it is strictly necessary because dealing with a manipulator can become dangerous. In any case, whatever the decision you make, always ask an external person for help, even better if they are qualified.

DON'T FALL INTO THEIR TRAP

Most of us come across instances where others seek to manipulate our thoughts, attitudes, or actions and take advantage of them to their advantage. In one such case, you fail to understand the true motive. The person mentally dominates you, and you step into the pit. Often this emotional abuse costs you a lot when you make some critical decisions under another person's control, and you only realize when it is too late.

You have to be cautious when a relationship sounds too good to be true. They are showering you with compassion, gratitude, admiration, congratulations, and affection. You feel like you live in a dream where everything seems perfect. They don't give you a reason to worry. You simply cannot find any flaws in them. Also, if anything goes wrong, they can begin to weep or feel sorry. You can become the object of extreme intimacy and have passion for the fairy tale.

Because you began the relationship with love bombing, all of a sudden you start feeling ignored. You are receiving gratitude, presents, and recognition, but rarely. You feel like you're losing your grip or want someone else in your life. You get another gift from them, the moment you make up your mind to move on, making the decision difficult. They are trying to get leverage over you in situations like these. For most instances, amazingly, this works, and you end up going back to them

Individuals often succeed in manipulating their victims after intermittent reinforcement. We can avoid behaving in the same way while fighting back or by demanding an answer. The explanation is that they are taking complete care of you now, so there is no need for intermittent strengthening because we no longer need it. Manipulators have many different faces, and in the same manner, they can use many ways to get things done. The person may make a plan, and later deny it, so that you begin to doubt your perception. They make you feel bad when you try to make them aware of their promise. They can employ shallow sympathy and burst into crocodile tears. Eventually, you end up trusting them and even doubting whether you listened correctly.

You can't believe the smiling faces that seem confident and strong are the same manipulative people, that often have self-serving prejudices, so they think less of other person's feelings. They have a reason to look for others who affirm them and make them even feel superior.

STEER STRAIGHT WHEREVER POSSIBLE

A manipulator's actions typically vary according to the situation they're in. For instance, a manipulator may speak rudely to one person, and act respectfully towards another the next moment. When you see these extremes frequently in a person, it would be advisable to stay away from them. And you have to communicate with this guy. That will prevent you from becoming a deceptive victim.

One way to identify a manipulator is to see how a person is behaving in different circumstances and before different people. Although we all have a sense of this sort of social distinction, some psychological manipulators seem to dwell in extremes habitually, being highly polite to one person, and gross to another - or helpless at one moment, and fiercely violent at another. If you frequently experience this form of behavior from an adult, keep a healthy distance away, and avoid interacting with the person unless you have to. As described earlier, there are nuanced and deep-seated causes for persistent psychological abuse. Saving them is not your job.

There are some circumstances in which you can't fully leave a relationship-usually when that person is a parent or an extended family member. You probably cannot go cold turkey unless the individual causes serious harm or psychological damage. Next, you need to accept this person completely for who they are and change your relationship standards accordingly. If they were someone you needed validation from before, then you would have to quit looking for their validation. Recognize that their advice is not something you need in your life. When they keep offering it, you can thank them for it, and then politely dump it. When setting these limits, be as discreet as you can, and do not tell the other person you are setting them apart. Creating this shift at your end will take some time, and when you get upset with the other person in the process, you will have to deal with their reaction on top of that.

Knowing this will drain your energy a little bit, set limits around the time you spend with that person. If you've been hanging out every Saturday with your manipulating mother-in-law, cut it down to once a month and plan something for that day so that there is a definite end time for your hangout.

CALL THEM OUT ON THEIR ACTIONS

Manipulators are always difficult to deal with, but the worst are discreet manipulators. They will stay cool as a cucumber when confronted, and yet rigid and unbending. You may start to get frustrated when you start seeing their faulty reasoning. When you keep fighting with them, you'll find it hard not to raise your voice a bit. You will start looking like the irrational one, and they will try to take back control in remaining calm, based on their "maturity."

Defending yourself is tempting and trying to get the other person to see what is going on. But a true manipulator will not change their tune, and the more you give in to that urge to protect yourself, the more they will twist your words more. It will not be long before you get stuck in this twisted web of myths and false expectations. If you are in a situation with a true manipulator, the two goals for any conflict that is taking place should be to resolve and leave, whether that means leaving the current conversation or exiting the relationship. Avoid threats, accusations, losing patience, accusing the other person of coercion, or become excessively emotional. Stick to honest, factual, and respectful declarations when you speak.

Some things require a high degree of intelligence, flexibility, or self-discipline when dealing with a manipulative person. You might not have the self-control to react without losing your temper and making things worse. If that's the case, accept this about yourself and take extra steps to avoid a tense confrontation (invite a mediator into the conversation, for example, or send an email instead of meeting in person, so you have time to think through what you say).

For me, it can cause a bit of tension to deal with someone who loses their temper. I needed to have a friend with me to feel secure in circumstances where there were a lot of blow-up risks. However, much as I wished I could handle the conflict myself, I realized that I wasn't quite in a position to do so. I would have felt a lot of needless discomforts if I had failed to acknowledge this about myself because of my decision to act better than I was. Wouldn't you be better at handling the problem than you are? Others will be attacking the vulnerable points and trying to make it seem like the problem will be easier for you to deal with than it is. Do not equate your reaction to someone else's reaction in one case.

IGNORE WHAT THEY DO AND SAY

It is intended to ignore the dishonest men. These people flip flop over things, they're slippery when you try to keep them accountable, they promise support that never comes, they're always making you feel guiltyeverything you don't want in person. The greatest mistake you can make when dealing with a dishonest person is trying to correct him or her. You sink deeper into their pit, by correcting them. Humans will use anger and misunderstanding to lure you into a confrontation. We want to make you feel nervous so that they can see how you tick. When they learn the triggering factors, you will use them to affect your actions. A smarter approach is to ignore them entirely. Only erase them from your life if you can't delete them instantly-even if they're a supervisor, coworker, or member of the family and then carry on doing your own thing anyway.

TOUCH THEIR CENTRE OF GRAVITY

Manipulative people actively take advantage of their tactics against you. Through your enemies, they will become enemies, and turn them against you. They will dangle some small reward in front of you and make you chase it relentlessly-they're going to take it away any time you get close to it. You will forever keep past acts up against you and on and on. Avoid letting those who exploit you, by using their tactics against you. Switch the tables instead. Build your plan and hit them where it hurts. When you are forced to deal with a dishonest person who, no matter how hard you try to avoid them, tries to make your life miserable, your only choice is to find their center of gravity and destroy it. This center may be associates, followers, or subordinates to the deceptive individual. It may be a high-level talent or advanced knowledge of a particular area. They can manage it as a particular resource.

Figure out what their center of gravity is and make it yours anyway. Creating alliances with those close to them, hiring people to replace them with their skill sets and knowledge base, or siphoning away their precious assets. This will throw them off balance and push them to concentrate on managing their life, not yours.

BELIEVE IN YOUR DECISION

You know better than anyone else what is best for your future. Many people are going around asking for the views of other people on anything. "What do I want to do with my life? "What am I fantastic at? "Where am I, then?", avoid searching for other people's validation and describe it yourself. Define yourself. Believe in yourself. What distinguishes winners from losers is not the ability to listen to other people's opinions; it's the ability to listen to one's own opinions. You prevent dishonest people from influencing your life by setting up your values and keeping them tightly onto them. This will serve as a firewall to your convictions, keeping manipulators ostracized and out of your way.

TRY NOT TO FIT RIGHT IN

Keep reinventing yourself. One myth is the belief that continuity is somehow admirable or related to achievement. Manipulative people want you to be consistent so that they can count on you to advance their agendas. They want you to show up at 9 am every day and work at minimum wage for them. We want you to come home on time and make them feel good about themselves and clean the house.

Consistent assembly lines. The prison is uniform. Consistency is how they trap you in a shell. It's their way of manipulating you. The only way to stop being exploited is by consciously going against all the barriers other people seek to create for you. Let go of trying to blend in. Instead, look to stand out. Act different in some way, and never remain the same for too long. By design, personal growth needs a lack of consistency. Constant change is expected to achieve constant reinvention.

AVOID CONCESSION

Guilt is an emotion of no use, but this is a powerful tool. Guilt is one of those weapons that would be used against you by dishonest men. They will make you feel bad for past defeats and small mistakes, or they will make you feel guilty for being overconfident and prideful. They'll use it against you if you spend time feeling happy or sure of yourself. One will never feel too good about themselves; they would claim. Another tool that is being used against you by manipulators is doubt. They will work to instill within you a sense of self-doubt-doubts about your ability and your worth. Their ultimate goal is to take you off balance and make you second guess yourself. Within this state of confusion, manipulators gain control. Their power is getting greater and they are twice as likely to convince you to compromise on your principles, ambitions, and yourself.

Simple solution-avoid feeling guilty. When it comes to your own life, you owe nothing to anyone. You deserve to feel good about yourself and to be stunned by your achievements. You deserve to have a good sense of confidence and self-belief in what you do. It is neither moral nor enlightened to compromise on either of these issues. This is then the path to self-destruction.

NEVER ASK FOR PERMISSION

Asking for forgiveness is better than asking for permission. The problem is that we have been conditioned to ask for permission constantly. As a boy, we had to ask for everything we wanted — to be fed, changed, and burped. We had to ask permission to go to the bathroom, and we had to wait to eat lunch at a designated time and wait for our turn to play with toys. As a result, most people expect to seek permission.

Employees around the world are waiting for a promotion and waiting for their turn to talk. Most are so used to being chosen that they sit in meetings in silence, afraid to talk out of turn or even lift their hands. It's a different way of living.

What if you did it what you wanted to, whenever you want? And what if you quit being too worried about politeness and feel relaxed with others? What if, instead, you live your life exactly the way you want to live it? These are all things you can do whenever you want.

Manipulative people want you to feel constrained by some abstract law or principle that says you can't behave freely without consulting an authority figure or a party. The reality is that at any given moment, you can miss this feeling of confinement. You will continue living a completely different life today than you lived yesterday. Your decision is yours.

BUILD A GREATER SENSE OF MISSION

Destiny driven people aren't easily fooled. The reason manipulators in this world tend to prosper is that so many people lead a purposeless life. If there is no reason in your life, you cannot believe anything. They will do anything. Because, somehow, nothing matters. People who lack intent waste time. There is no rhyme or explanation behind how they live their lives. We don't know where to go, or why they are here. They remain busy to avoid the desperate feeling of emptiness growing inside them. This profession and loneliness empower deceptive individuals.

Every minute, a sucker is born. When you are constantly distracted, consuming pointless stuff, trying to stay busy-you are the sucker. By peddling meaningless knowledge and events, manipulators manipulate purposeless people. The only way to escape this, is by cultivating a sense of destiny. Destiny is doing away with distraction. The manipulators can't hurt you because you think for yourself. They cannot confuse you or lead you astray.

TAKE NEW OPPORTUNITIES

The universe wants to put your eggs in one bowl. People all around you ask you to lock yourself in on decisions such as a mortgage, a car payment, a secure relationship, a single position at the office. They want you staked down to a single choice for the rest of your life. Nowadays, it is also looked down upon for being optimistic. Staying hungry is also seen as a sign of weakness. Why can't you just be happy with what you have? Why should you be so greedy? If you show a desire for more, this is what dishonest people would ask you. They will call you vain, greedy, prideful. They'll make you feel cold and uncomfortable like you're heartless and inhumane. The reality is that they want to keep you in your place. They want you to stay at the same job and spend the rest of your life living in the same place. They want you and the structures they control to remain dependent upon them.

The only way to stay autonomous is to look for new possibilities and build new ones actively. Continue applying for new jobs, continue to start at new companies, developing new partnerships, and seeking new experiences.

AVOID BEING AN INFANT

When you get fooled by someone, shame on them. When you're fooled by someone ten times, you're an idiot. Avoid letting manipulators walk all over you. Nobody feels sorry for you, and you're always being humiliated. Have enough self-consciousness and reverence for yourself to say no to dishonest men.

You cannot just walk around life, blaming the troubles on others. You cannot simply walk away from the people trying to control you, either. Yes, some people are negative and manipulative. And yes, these people will try to use you. Yet, that doesn't mean that you have a free pass to make mistakes. Without your permission, no-one can control you. You are to blame for your achievements and defeats. If others outstrip you, it's your fault, not theirs, so be smart. Learn from your wrongs. You don't want to fall victim to the same slippery person again and again. Slice them free. Remove them from your life. Commit to connecting yourself with like-minded people who will not be exploiting you.

BETTING ON YOURSELF

Take a gamble on the one thing in life that you can control yourself. Too many people restrict themselves to considering only external factors when making difficult decisions. They consider the financial consequences of a situation and its relationships. Yet they fail to acknowledge the impact on their satisfaction and sense of self-worth their choice would have. As a result, when they should be taking chances on themselves, they take chances on other people. Then, they wonder why they are unhappy.

If you just take chances on strangers and things, you put yourself at the mercy of those people and things. It makes you weak and ready to be exploited. You should take chances on yourself instead. In any tough situation you find yourself facing, don't ask questions like, "Who's the right one to side with?" or "What choice would be more likely to succeed?" rather, say, "What am I most likely to do?" so go out and do that. For example, if you face an opportunity to start your own company or keep working at the same dead-end job, don't keep the job just because the pay is stable. Don't just leave because the relationships are slightly unpleasant. You are betting on external factors when you do so, which is a mistake. Betting on yourself is a safer plan.

You would never regret making a bet on yourself. You will, of course, have to take full responsibility for any mistakes that you make. Sure, you need to stick to a higher standard. Yet you, too, must be solely responsible for your victories. You will continue to rise and achieve greater and higher rates of success.

STOP GETTING EMOTIONALLY ATTACHED TO THEM

All you do with a manipulator is fake. Every fight you have been through is your fault. Manipulation will wreak havoc on your feelings. You go from crying to being furious in a short period of time, then to feeling guilty and indignant. Then you feel sorry you did not stick up for yourself. You are ashamed to let them do that to you again, and your emotions are more stable once you've left a manipulator.

Life is a journey into an adventure. On the way, many people come to give us company at various times, for a certain amount of time and leave after they play their part in our lives. There is no problem with the people coming and going, but the difficulties occur when you are emotionally attached to the people and feel powerless, tense, and worried when the relationship ends, especially with an emotional manipulator. Therefore, if you want to stay healthy and make progress in life, you need to resolve the emotional connection as soon as possible. There is no doubt that some individuals will become the driving force for you to move towards the path you have chosen but when being separated from them, you should be careful not to get distracted. You need to make judicious use of the relationships. Be attached to individuals with a detached approach and take care of them to create a confident atmosphere. However, when you push them out of your life for being a manipulator with another relationship waiting for you, do not be dependent on that person for your growth by stopping your life. You need to re-focus on your journey, leaving behind memories.

Handling emotional connection measures the degree of sophistication of one's journey down the desired direction, and its gravity. Treat yourself to the moments you share with friends. Learn from them, love them, and look after them, but don't make them your walking sticks. Much of the time, people are usually afraid to lose anyone because of their incapacity to go on in life alone. So, if you dare walk alone on the chosen path, you no longer have to be dependent on emotional connections.

INSPIRING THEM

Using all the experience you've acquired to become your best self, help others to become their best. If you are having trouble improving their behavior, work with a counselor. It can be very difficult to change their behavior, and you may not be able to do it on your own. A psychologist or therapist may help him recognize habits that need to be altered and discuss the feelings that are behind him. These will also help him develop new, healthy behaviors.

TELL THEM "YOU'RE OK."

This begins with you not responding to their techniques anymore. If you don't want to something, you say "no," or you speak your mind even though they don't like it. Work on feeling okay with how negatively they may react. When they're not yours, don't pick them up.

You can only keep your act under control. That's crucial because you won't be able to alter a manipulator's behavior, however, you can avoid being their victim. That happens when you start saying, "no." The first step in breaking the cycle is to recognize that they manipulate us because we allow it and do not refuse to be manipulated. Manipulators are good at what they do, so watch out for their reaction. You would probably say or do things that tug at the heartstrings. Stand firm in saying "no," realizing we are taking the first step to free ourselves from their power.

LET GO OF NASTY RELATIONSHIPS

Toxic partnerships can be hard to let go of. Many people find themselves caught in a cycle of returning to relationships that are not good for them. This just creates a cycle of hurt and grief. Toxic relationships can be let go of. Psychologists have worked with people who have had this issue to be able to write a whole handbook about it. The very first step to getting out of a toxic relationship is admitting to yourself that the relationship isn't perfect. You can try and note down explanations of the sign indicating a toxic relationship. It's called 'cognitive dissonance' if you notice that uncomfortable feeling in the back of your mind, and it's your brain trying to protect you from what you know is true. Take note of the things that make you feel this way in a relationship. The first step is to recognize that your relationship is toxic. You have to be conscious of all the things that affect you before you can truly be free.

Relationships are a side lane. Two people are involved in the relationship, meaning that two people are involved in all the disagreements, arguments, and behavior. You cannot fully take the blame yourself. If you blame yourself for all of the relationship problems, you'll find yourself going back to trying to fix them. Recognize that both parties are sometimes at fault for a dysfunctional relationship. Recognize your responsibilities, but your responsibilities alone. Within a toxic relationship, you don't need to be concerned with anyone else's issues. There's no need to hoist it on yourself because you aren't to blame.

Some of the best things you can do while trying to let go of a controlling partner is to cut off communication. Keeping in touch would just make letting go harder. This involves seeking out toxic people that are no longer in your life by scrolling through their social media or questioning how they are doing through mutual friends. You should still follow your intuition when it comes to cutting people out of your life, according to Sarah Newman, M.A. Although it may sound drastic, Newman advises loosening the bonds when it comes to a toxic relationship. You need to be in a position to move on, where you can feel optimistic about the lack of touch, rather than pain.

Mariana Bockarova, Ph.D., says that closure is one of the best things to move on from a manipulative and broken relationship. Bockarova understands that closure will help people reconstruct their whole lives safely and positively. Thus, one way to help you let go of a toxic relationship is to find closure. Healing comes from inside for many people by considering all the ways the relationship went wrong in the first place. Writing one more letter or making the other party recognize the toxicity will provide closure for some. Whatever it is, the closure might help you move on.

The most important thing in quitting and letting go of an abusive relationship is having someone there to catch you if you fall. It can be unsettling to let go, especially if it is a long-term one. Keep in contact with friends and relatives who will support you through the more stressful moments. This will also help to keep you accountable when it comes to not reaching out those you've cut off. Aid networks are essential in allowing dysfunctional partnerships to go away. Don't fear reaching out to people who love you the most.

DEVELOP A STRONG MINDSET

Although one toxic person may use coercion and lies, another may have recourse to intimidation and incivility. If you're not careful, it can take a serious toll on your life because of people like this. Nevertheless, mentally healthy people deal skillfully with manipulative people. They refuse to give away their strength, and no matter who surrounds them, they continue to be their best self.

Putting a label on emotions reduces their intensity. So, whether you feel sad, nervous, frustrated, or afraid, confess it — at least to yourself. Pay attention also to how those emotions can affect your choices. You can be less likely to take chances when you are feeling nervous. You may get more impulsive when you're excited. Increasing the understanding of the feelings will reduce the risk that you will make emotionally driven, unreasonable decisions.

Listing your emotions is just part of the fight — you need skills to control your emotions as well. Think of your current abilities to cope. Should you eat something when you're nervous? Should you drink to keep yourself calm? When you're mad, will you show it to your friends? If you're anxious, will you stay at home? These conventional strategies can make you feel better right now, but they will make you feel worse in the long run. Search for long-term coping strategies that are perfect for you. Keep in mind that what works for one person doesn't always work for another, and you need to figure out what's best for you to manage your emotions. Experimenting with various coping mechanisms to figure out what works for you, deep breathing, exercising, meditating, reading, painting, and spending time in nature are only a few techniques that could help.

The way you think has an impact on how you feel and how you behave. You are deprived of intellectual energy by saying things like, "I can't take this," or "I'm such an idiot." Pay attention to what you think. You'll probably note recurring trends and themes. Maybe you're telling yourself things you feel uncomfortable about doing. Or maybe you're telling yourself you're not in control of your life.

Respond with something more constructive to the unproductive and unreasonable feelings. Instead of saying, "I'm going to screw this up," think, "This is my chance to shine, and I'm going to do my best." Changing the interactions you're having with yourself can be the most instrumental thing you can do to improve your existence. Changing your attitude is the only way to teach your brain to think differently. Do tough things — and keep doing them even though you don't think you should. You will be demonstrating to yourself that you are stronger than you think. Set up healthy daily habits too. Practice appreciation, exercise, get plenty of sleep and follow a balanced diet for the brain and body to be at its best. Seek out individuals who inspire you to be your best and create an atmosphere that helps you develop a balanced lifestyle.

Many positive habits won't work if you practice them alongside your bad habits. It is like eating donuts on a treadmill while you're running. Pay attention to your bad habits (we all have them) that rob you of the mental strength. Whether you feel bad for yourself or envy the success of other people, it takes only one or two to keep you stuck in life. Once you realize your bad habits, spend your energy replacing them with healthier alternatives. You will then be able to step out of the hamster wheel and actively work towards your goals.

Just as it takes time and practice to become physically strong, it takes dedication to build mental strength. The key to feeling your best and reaching your most significant potential is to build mental muscle.

GIVE YOURSELF CONSTRUCTIVE SELF-APPRAISAL ALL DAY LONG

An emotional manipulator will tarnish your mood, so make sure you restore yourself during the day with uplifting self-talks. Each of us has a set of messages that keep playing in our minds over and over. Our responses to life and its circumstances are represented by this internal dialog or personal commentary. One way to recognize, encourage, and maintain optimism, hope, and happiness is to fill our minds with optimistic self-talking consciously. Far too often, because of our manipulative partner, the self-talk pattern that we have formed is negative. We recall the derogatory things our friends, parents, siblings, or teachers told us as children. We remember other children's adverse reactions, which undermined the way we felt about ourselves. Such messages have been playing in our minds over the years, strengthening our feelings of rage, fear, guilt, and hopelessness.

Some of the most important approaches used in dealing with those suffering from depression are to determine the root of these messages and to work with the individual to "overwrite" them deliberately. If a person learned he was worthless as a child, we'd show him how special he is. If a person has learned to expect disasters and catastrophic events while growing up, we will teach her a better way to predict the future.

Check the exercise below. Within your head, write down some of the negative thoughts that hinder your desire to resolve your circumstance. Whenever possible, be precise, and include everyone you know who contributed to it. Now, take a moment to consciously combat the negative messages in your life with constructive truths. Don't give up when you're not quick to find them, because there are always truths for every negative message which will help override them. So keep looking until you find them.

You can get a negative message replaying in your mind if you make a mistake. You might have been told as a child, "You're never going to amount to anything," or "You can't do anything right." When you make a mistake, and you will because we all do - you can choose to overwrite that message with a positive one, such as "I choose to accept and grow from my mistake" or "As I learn from my mistakes, I become a better person." Good self-conversation isn't self-deception. It's not looking at circumstances through rose tinted glasses, instead, it is about acknowledging the truth in situations and within you. One of the fundamental truths is that you will be making mistakes. It is unfair to expect perfection in yourself or someone else. It's also unrealistic to expect no difficulties in life, whether by your actions or by pure circumstances.

When adverse events or mistakes occur, positive self-talk is aimed at bringing the positive out of the negative to help you do better, go further, or simply move forward. The practice of constructive self-talk is also the mechanism that helps you to discover in any given situation the hidden happiness, hope, and joy.

STAY OBSERVANT

If you know that you are a target, you must be observant at all times. In other words, we all need to stay observant. Everybody is a prime target of manipulation. People will come to you to take advantage of your situation. Staying observant means that you can look at people and read their intentions. As we have observed, NLP professionals will use their extraction techniques to try and gauge our thoughts and beliefs. If you wish to stop those individuals from controlling your life and thinking process, you must stay aware. Always try to remember that there is someone out there who may be looking to take control of your thoughts.

BE SECRETIVE

Do not be a person who gives out your information to everyone. A manipulative person can only control you if they know something about you. If the manipulator does not have any information about you, they may not have any valid reasons to control your life. If you want to stay on your feet and stop all the people who come to your life to control you, you must learn to stop them by blocking their quest to gain knowledge about your life.

LEARN TO CONTROL YOUR EMOTIONS

NLP experts do not need you to speak for them to gather information. NLP experts rely more on the emotional clues that you send out during conversations. You must learn how to control your expressive and physiological aspects of emotions. The physiological aspects of emotion include the bodily changes that take place when you are emotional. For instance, the sweating of hands when you are anxious or afraid. Such physiological changes may sell you out to the person who wants to get more information to manipulate you. The expressive aspect of emotions includes bodily actions that you display when you are emotional. A good example would be running away when you are afraid. Although you may choose to stay, the actions of running away or choosing to fight are an expressive part of your emotions that NLP experts may use to gather more information about your past.

AVOID ISOLATION

Try as much as possible to ensure that you do not allow a manipulative person to isolate you. When you are isolated, you are weak and vulnerable. Most manipulative people gain control during moments of weakness, such as isolation.

Conclusion

There has been lots of discussion about dark psychology, how and in which situations it is practiced most commonly and what the factors hidden behind it are. This is also considered to be a dark side of human nature, which is seldom exposed. Every human being, no matter how nice and positive they are, are always going to be evil in someone else's eyes. For the person whom you made suffer, you are evil, even if you deny it. Every person must evaluate him or herself and see if any of the hazardous or negative elements are found in them. You have to keep fighting your dark side so that it does not take control over you completely. Once you know to keep off that side, you will be able to identify it in others as well and can prevent yourself from falling prey to it. One must be aware of its indications and related signs so that people who have the qualities of dark psychology can be avoided. If you have fallen prey to dark psychology, then there is a chance for you to regain normality by assessing and evaluating yourself or by seeking medical advice.

Remember that deception is not always practiced on other people. We can often self-deceive to preserve our self-esteem. Telling ourselves that we can achieve certain goals when all the evidence points to the fact that we can't, is a healthy form of deception, but self-deception can lead to serious delusions.

Whatever happens in the novice stages of your path to becoming a master of manipulation and persuasion, you must remember your end goal. Ask yourself in the beginning why you want to do this and keep coming back to that when it gets hard. Never give up; you are to master these skills.

I hope that through this book, you have realized that brainwashing, manipulation, and persuasion depends greatly on an authoritative command of words. You might be able to list twenty manipulation techniques from memory; you may be able to get someone with little psychic resistance to go with your ideas.

You may have gotten to the end of the book — and you may have all the knowledge necessary to manipulate people — but you are just beginning when it comes to putting this all into practice.

Also, remember manipulation is classified into positive and negative (Egocentric and Malicious). The study shows how to avoid negative manipulators and try as hard as possible to stay in your lane. Work on the positive aspect of manipulation to help yourself and help others — best of luck!

www.ingramcontent.com/pod-product-compliance
Lightning Source LLC
Chambersburg PA
CBHW071545080526
44588CB00011B/1795